What Our Readers Have Said...

Applicability

"These books are great tools that should be used as guidelines for our everyday supervisory practices. You need to take the time to do a short self-evaluation when reading them."

•

"The Pinpoint Training Series delivers information that could be used in a lot different areas."

•

"The things and problems we deal with everyday are discussed in these books."

Convenience

"I like this because I can take them with me to read at a convenient time. I feel the little time I have to spend in the office is best use on activities that directly relate to revenue opportunities. I like the short amount of time it takes to keep up with these."

•

"I prefer the self-study approach; it fits in with my schedule."

•

"I like the fact that the format allows the books to be reviewed as time permits. All work has been conducted on personal, evening/weekend time."

•

"Easy to use... if you put the time into it."

Challenge

"My thought is that the real value of these books comes into effect when doing the action plans."

•

"I like the fact that the format allows assignments to be reviewed as time permits."

Clarity

"Short and sweet. These books are easy to comprehend."

•

"Easy to use, understand, and reference if needed."

Relevance

"I have enjoyed reading these books. They are relevant to today's work environment and the ongoing change in the way we manage our workforce."

•

"I believe the contents of the Pinpoint series are excellent. It causes one to reflect on the daily dynamics in working with oneself as well as with management and peers."

Planning to Maximize Performance

Pinpoint Leadership Skill Development Training Series

TIMOTHY F. BEDNARZ

MAJORIUM
BUSINESS PRESS

Pinpoint Leadership Skill Development Training Series
"Planning to Maximize Performance"
Timothy F. Bednarz

Graphic design: Monika Pawlak

Majorium Business Press
2025 Main Street
Stevens Point, WI 54481
715.342.1018 • 800.654.4935

ISBN 978-1-882181-67-4

Printed in the United States of America

Introduction

The Pinpoint Leadership Skill Development Training Series is designed for targeted training and education regarding increased improvement in a specific skill or competency.

Each book within this series is designed to be easy to use, understand and apply to your job. It can be used as a basis for training individuals, as a discussion guide or as a personal training tool.

Each chapter within this book discusses a specific concept. When you have completed all eight chapters you should have a 360° perspective of the topic.

Additionally, each chapter is divided into specific sections:

- The first section provides you with an overview of the topic
- The Implications section discusses why the concept is important, and why it is important to learn and apply.
- The Strategies, Tips & Techniques to Apply section teaches how to use and apply the particular concept to your work.
- The Points to Ponder section gives you something to think about or to be discussed with a group setting. These are questions not meant to be immediately answered, but to be pondered over time.
- The Training Activity section provides you with the tools to transfer what you have learned to your job. It is designed to help create an action plan to effectively apply the concept.

Each of the topics in this series is time-tested and proven in the marketplace. They have been used by thousands of employees as training tools. Many of the users have commented that what made these books valuable, was the ability to refer to them when a problem surfaced. They indicated that they remembered reading about the exact problem. They referred back to these books and found an appropriate solution.

You will find them equally valuable as a resource in your professional development library.

Table of Contents

LEARNING OBJECTIVES:

- To identify the elements and factors that encompass the realm of performance planning.
- To understand the implications and ramifications that enhances or diminishes individual performance planning.
- How to apply effective strategies to enhance individual performance planning.
- To analyze cause and effect relationships and the subsequent impact due to ineffective performance planning.
- How performance planning impacts decision making.

1

Performance Plans Transform a Leader's Vision into Reality

When developing their annual plans to meet the goals and expectations of senior management, leaders reach beyond what is expected. Leaders search for every possible way to motivate their subordinates with their passion for what everyone can achieve.

A leader's vision distinguishes him or her from other managers. As such, in carrying it out they constantly seek ways to overachieve and motivate and encourage others to stretch their personal limits and capabilities. They are enabled to do this through planning. They use their performance plan for personal motivation and for driving others to achieve and succeed. This passion overcomes the daily frustrations and barriers that hinder individuals' moving forward. Leaders see these barriers as opportunities to bring out the best in their subordinates.

IMPLICATIONS – WHAT THIS MEANS TO YOU

It is important for leaders to understand that in order to motivate and drive their organization to success they need to have a vision of what they and others can do. Their vision and passion becomes the engine driving their plans, goals and objectives. Only by utilizing its thrust are they able to stretch the overall performance of their unit.

STRATEGIES, TIPS & TECHNIQUES TO APPLY

Leaders have a vision of what their organizational unit is capable of achieving. It is a view shared with senior management as to what they envision the company can achieve in the future. This mutual vision becomes a shared passion for turning seemingly impossible objectives into reality.

It Starts with a Vision

Before leaders can solidify their vision with performance plans, they must look at his or her area of responsibility and specifically identify what is possible for the unit to achieve. This can include assessments of structure, profitability, productivity and operations. This analysis of the unit's potential drives its goals, objectives and performance.

Leaders Communicate and Share Their Vision

Leaders don't keep their vision to themselves—they communicate and share it with passion. This passion compels associates and subordinates to embrace it as their own. It empowers them to work together to realize its rewards. As the vision is shared, all have ownership in its progress and outcomes.

Leaders Point the Way to Achievement of Their Vision

A vision to a leader is the summit of the mountain he or she wishes to climb. No matter what happens during the climb, they keep their eyes on the objective. This spurs them on toward achieving it.

Once the goal is firmly established and the vision is defined, leaders point the way to its attainment. They identify the best course of action and create a specific roadmap for their subordinates to follow. This entails the development of several critical elements, including:

Timelines

A vision is not accomplished in the short-term. It can take several years for a team to actually achieve the vision a leader creates. This requires long-range planning. Since time frames are often expanded along the way, modifications and adaptations may be needed as particular circumstances change.

Once a long-range strategy is established, short-term plans need to be developed and squared with the leader's annual plans. This is readily accomplished because his or her plans will exceed those set by upper management.

Resources and Requirements

Once plans and timelines are set, leaders must identify the resources and operational requirements needed to achieve their vision. This information is typically incorporated into their long-range strategy. It is readjusted yearly in order to be incorporated into annual performance plans.

Beyond necessary resources, consideration must be given to the organizational unit's additional requirements for developing and accomplishing their shared vision over time.

Tasks, Roles and Assignments

Leaders adapt their organizational units to fit into their long-range plans. Their planning aligns the unit with assigning, adapting and modifying tasks, roles and assignments to the attainment of their vision.

Each responsibility, task and role must be linked to the plan timeline and have appropriate operational resources assigned. Each subordinate is assigned specific goals and objectives. This assures a total understanding of what is expected. Responsibility is greatly increased when goals and objectives are clearly defined.

Follow-up and Support

As it is essential for every member of the organizational unit to share the leader's vision, follow-up mechanisms for each assignment need to be developed and placed into a time frame. This assures each task is completed on time and as planned. Additionally, leaders plan for ways to encourage their unit members to support one another in the accomplishment of tasks, responsibilities and roles required to achieve the leader's vision.

POINTS TO PONDER — SOMETHING TO THINK ABOUT

1. Have you ever imagined what is possible for you and your team to accomplish if given the opportunity?
2. Are you motivated and driven by a personal vision? Explain.

TRAINING ACTIVITY — APPLICATION & ACTION PLAN

1. If you have not already done so, define your personal vision and write it down.
2. Determine ways that you can effectively communicate and share your vision with your employees.
3. Develop a long-range plan that leads to the achievement of your vision.
    - How long will it take?
    - What needs to be done?
    - Who will do it?
    - What resources and support do they need?
    - What tasks, roles and responsibilities need to be defined and assigned to accomplish your vision?
4. What do you need to do to follow up on and support your employees' efforts to accomplish your vision?

2

Formulating Performance Plans

A performance plan differs from a conventional plan in that it is a proactive document. It is designed for continuous use throughout the year as a guide and reference tool to direct the leader and his or her unit's activities. The primary purpose of a performance plan is to create results and maximize performance.

Managers often produce an annual performance plan only to give senior management what they want to see. Leaders view performance planning as an opportunity to review and analyze actual past performance. It gives them the means to identify ways to improve their personal and organizational unit's overall performance and productivity.

IMPLICATIONS – WHAT THIS MEANS TO YOU

Managers as leaders actively use their performance plan to drive the unit's as well as their own performance. They continually reference their performance plan as a roadmap throughout the year to guide and direct their activities and courses of action as well as those of their subordinates.

STRATEGIES, TIPS & TECHNIQUES TO APPLY

Leaders work and plan under the direction of senior management. They define overall strategic company goals and plans. Senior management also forms operational and tactical strategies directing the company's activities during the year. Typically leaders are responsible for specific aspects of the operational and tactical plans. Their performance plans are directly linked to their assigned goals and objectives. How leaders accomplish these goals and objectives is self-defined. This is where they are given an opportunity to shine.

As was discussed in the previous lesson, leaders are driven by a vision of what is possible, not expected. In formulating a performance plan, leaders begin with an initial preparation before it is formally written and executed. This preliminary process includes:

Collecting and Correlating Data

Leaders collect and correlate the information and data they developed during a review of their organizational unit's prior performance. This provides a complete picture of the unit's successes and weaknesses. It helps pinpoint how successes can be capitalized on, and identifies the problems and issues that must be resolved to maximize the unit's performance.

Leaders ensure their plans coincide with their vision. This is necessary if their vision is to be attained. They analyze and make sure plans can be incorporated into their overall goals and objectives.

The information collected from these two planning activities provides reliable insight and direction. It shapes how performance plans are to be formulated and becomes the foundation for all future performance plans.

Brainstorming

Leaders obtain input and feedback from all members of their unit. This strategy works to bring individual members "on board." It greatly increases the probability they will accept the plan and implement the necessary strategies to make it successful.

Leaders use brainstorming to get reliable feedback. They use this feedback to creatively approach the development of their performance plan. They need to "think outside of the box" to view their goals and objectives creatively and without bias. Brainstorming accomplishes this by encouraging entrepreneurial thinking. Then leaders can easily define the issues concerning maximizing unit performance from various perspectives.

The purpose of brainstorming is not only to identify ways to achieve goals and complete tasks. It is used as a method to seek out information and ideas for exceeding normal expectations. Leaders always look for ways to optimize performance and results. Effective brainstorming also helps them improve budgetary performance as it maximizes the use of assigned resources.

Formulating Plans

Throughout the preparation and brainstorming phases of planning, the performance plan begins to take shape. Senior management has assigned the overall goals and objectives. The feedback and the analysis of the organizational unit details what needs to be accomplished. From this information, assumptions can be made that will form the basis of the plan.

Leaders clarify the specific direction the organizational unit will take. The steps needed to achieve this direction are carefully outlined and detailed. Each step is then formulated into specific objectives along with the activities required to attain the chosen course of direction.

From this information, leaders assign specific tasks and responsibilities to each individual unit member. These assignments become part of the performance plan, assuring that all objectives will be accomplished.

Leaders make sure each subordinate assigned to a task or responsibility has the necessary resources to be successful. Additionally, each task and responsibility includes established milestones so subordinates understand exactly what they need to do, by when. Milestones provide leaders with performance standards to ensure assigned tasks and responsibilities are accomplished in a timely fashion. This allows for effective managing of the performance plan as well as making modifications when needed.

Formalizing Plans

The final step of performance planning is to formalize a written plan. This becomes the actual management tool that guides and directs the organizational unit in the accomplishment of its goals and objectives.

The degree to which plans need to be refined will vary according to company standards. However, leaders make sure their plan clearly and precisely details the goals and objectives of the entire organizational unit. They write these in clear, easily understood language. Plans also include a timeline plotting each task, responsibility and milestone. Each time segment details the individual(s) responsible for specific tasks and their accomplishment and defines the resources to be allocated. All supporting data collected throughout the planning process is included to substantiate the plan, as well as the list of assumptions the plan is based upon.

POINTS TO PONDER — SOMETHING TO THINK ABOUT

1. Have you previously included your organizational unit's input into your performance planning process? Why or why not?
2. What is the most difficult part of your performance planning process? Why?

TRAINING ACTIVITY — APPLICATION & ACTION PLAN

1. Begin the development and formulation of your performance plan by following the steps detailed below.
2. Prepare for the planning process by reviewing the findings of your past performance reviews and detailing the ideas developed from your long-range plan to accomplish your vision.
3. Brainstorm your ideas, facts and findings with the members of your organizational department or unit. Solicit ideas and feedback. Agree upon ways to effectively and efficiently accomplish the assigned goals and objectives.
4. Based upon the findings, formulate your performance plan.

5. Develop a draft copy of your plan to review with the members of your organizational department or unit.
6. Come to a consensus on the final draft.

3

Effective Goal Setting Techniques

Leaders understand the importance of subordinate involvement throughout the goal setting process. They recognize that the involvement of all members of the organizational unit motivates them to accomplish the goals because they helped establish them.

Managers generally set their organizational goals without feedback or input from their subordinates. They often use plans and goals as directives subordinates are required to comply with irrespective of whether or not they are realistic or attainable.

Leaders on the other hand are not threatened by their employees' involvement in the planning process; instead they recognize and actively seek their input. This is because subordinates are the ones immersed in the front lines of the organization, and as such can offer real insights into improving productivity and performance. This adds a new dimension of thinking to the problem solving process.

Leaders also know many of their subordinates will not offer their insights unless specifically asked, and use the planning process as an opportunity to tap into this valuable resource.

IMPLICATIONS – WHAT THIS MEANS TO YOU

This is important to leaders because when they solicit ideas, expertise and feedback, they empower their subordinates. When subordinates offer ideas and suggestions, they have a personal interest in seeing that they are successfully implemented. This becomes a motivation to insure plans become reality.

STRATEGIES, TIPS & TECHNIQUES TO APPLY

The development of sound goals provides leaders an opportunity to motivate and engage their subordinates. The planning activities they participate in positively impact their personal lives and develop their professional skills. Subordinates are encouraged to fully participate, provide their personal insights and feedback and arrive at a consensus that benefits all involved.

Goal setting is accomplished by executing the following steps:

Review

Since most leaders function in organizational units that are part of a corporate structure, they work under the direction and goals set by senior management. They may be directed by the strategic goals of the company, a division, facility or department. This depends upon the level of management where the leader is situated.

When leaders review their goals, they again view them in terms of what is possible, and seek ways to apply their talents, skills and actions toward exceeding what is expected of them.

Brainstorm

Leaders use the available expertise and experience within their own organizational unit to solicit ideas, suggestions and feedback. They use this input to identify the best ways to achieve and exceed corporate goals and objectives.

Leaders clearly communicate to all members of the unit, in a factual and straightforward manner, the corporate goals, problems and issues they are facing. This lets everyone involved know what they must accomplish together. Leaders act as a facilitator, allowing subordinates to thoroughly discuss the problems and offer solutions and suggestions. All input is respectfully acknowledged and carefully considered.

List

The brainstorming session develops a series of ideas and suggestions as to how best to accomplish the goals and objectives assigned to the unit. All ideas are considered regardless of how irrational they may appear. Each idea is listed and recorded on a large sheet of paper or whiteboard for all to see. As members offer ideas and input, leaders make sure each individual is clearly heard, understood and respected.

Combine

Once all ideas are listed and recorded, leaders begin to combine all common ideas into a single concept. All members of the unit then need to arrive at a consensus regarding the wording of the unified concept.

Analyze

Leaders should ask all unit members to begin to analyze the distilled list, looking for gaps or information that is not pertinent. Gaps can then be filled and redundancies removed. All remaining ideas and suggestions should provide direction to the organizational unit for the complete accomplishment of their assigned goals.

Formalize

The items that remain on the refined list should be translated into goals for the organizational unit to accomplish. All members of the unit should arrive at a consensus regarding the language and specifics of each goal.

Prioritize

When all goals are formalized, the leader once again assumes the role of facilitator. In this capacity, he or she leads a discussion that prioritizes all goals in order of importance. All members of the unit should agree upon the order in which the goals are established.

Test

It is likely that more goals have been established than are practical for the organizational unit to accomplish.

The final step in the process is to test to identify which goals are realistic and attainable. Each should be evaluated against the time and resources available to the unit. As a group, the members of the organizational unit need to arrive at a consensus on the final list of goals. Leaders make sure that the final list goes beyond the comfort level of the unit. Doing this provides subordinates a structure in which to stretch their capabilities.

POINTS TO PONDER — SOMETHING TO THINK ABOUT

1. What methods do you use to develop goals for your organizational department or unit? Do you develop goals on your own or do you solicit feedback from your employees?
2. When your senior manager assigns you goals and objectives, do you identify ways you can not only successfully accomplish them but exceed expectations?

TRAINING ACTIVITY — APPLICATION & ACTION PLAN

Develop a goal setting procedure to use with your employees. Detail how you will implement the following steps:

- Reviewing
- Brainstorming
- Listing
- Combining
- Analyzing

- Formalizing
- Prioritizing
- Testing

4

Developing Definable and Realistic Objectives

Unrealistic and unattainable goals and objectives are a needless burden on employees. Unattainable goals drain the resources managers have at their disposal. While some managers believe impractical goals are a productive use of negative motivational techniques, research proves this approach ineffective in the long run. Ill-conceived goals raise anxiety and frustration levels, increasing burnout, negative attitudes and other counterproductive behaviors.

In the development of performance plans, leaders need to build in effective mechanisms to insure their organizational unit achieves and exceeds their goals and objectives. Leaders control how successful their units will be by how they define and establish these objectives. Techniques can be employed to vastly improve chances of success, just as a lack of concern and proper motivation will most often result in failure. Goals and objectives that are unattainable, unrealistic and overwhelming will never be accomplished.

IMPLICATIONS – WHAT THIS MEANS TO YOU

As their purpose is to insure the overall success of their organizational unit, it is vital for leaders to appreciate the importance of realistic goals. For years IBM used the philosophy of breaking down goals and objectives into smaller, more easily attained steps. This strategy proved a confidence and motivation builder, and stretched each individual's capability to succeed. Leaders can employ these same techniques to cultivate their employees and maximize the entire unit's success.

STRATEGIES, TIPS & TECHNIQUES TO APPLY

Objectives are the smaller steps needed to accomplish each goal. Implementing the following strategies can develop definable and realistic objectives. Selected procedures are similar to those previously addressed but with variations. All procedures must be repeated for each individual goal.

List

Leaders need to solicit the input and feedback of all members of their organizational unit in order to list and define all steps required to accomplish an objective. Care should be taken to break larger objectives down into smaller, more easily obtainable steps. This will make each step less overwhelming to the assigned individual(s). When tasks are seen as too large and overwhelming, employees tend to procrastinate and avoid accomplishing them. Success is built by steadily moving the process forward in smaller, incremental steps.

Prioritize

As was cited in the development of goals, all steps should be prioritized in order of their importance to accomplishing the objective. Leaders have their group arrive at a consensus as to the order of importance.

Responsibility

Every objective listed and agreed to by the members of the organizational unit should have a specific individual assigned to be responsible for its accomplishment. Leaders never assume these objectives will be reached automatically. It is a natural tendency to assume "someone else is handling it." Consequently no one accomplishes the objective. By assigning accomplishment responsibility to specific individuals, if and when the objectives are not being met, the leader knows who is to blame for the failure or oversight.

Resources

Once individuals have been assigned responsibility for the accomplishment of an objective, resources need to be assigned to that individual to ensure his or her success. In most corporate settings, a specific budget amount is allocated for each phase or objective of the performance plan.

Leaders may need to balance the utilization of assets to insure that every member of the organizational unit has adequate resources to accomplish all agreed upon goals and objectives. In many instances, resources may be assigned only for a period of time sufficient to accomplish the objective, then transferred to other unit members. In other cases, resources may need to be rationed or stretched to assure overall goals and objectives are met.

Milestones

Milestones should be created for each objective. These are essential benchmarks that individuals must achieve to assure that the objective is being met on schedule. Milestones also provide opportunities for leaders to receive feedback on the progress of the objective.

Performance Standards

At this point, individuals, budgets, resources and timelines have been assigned to each objective. Performance standards need to be established for each of these categories. These standards are written as the specific measures leaders will use to gauge the performance of each objective. Leaders then detail and discuss with each unit member how performance will be measured and evaluated. These standards and measurements are weighed against the experience and expertise of the individual assigned to a specific objective.

Reports and Follow-up

The final step is for leaders to determine the timing and frequency of progress reports to be submitted by each individual assigned to an objective. This will vary according to the objective and individual. Some will require more intensive assistance, while others may need only casual oversight. This will vary with leadership styles and by degree of confidence in the individual employee(s).

Leaders need to plan for effective follow-up with each individual assigned to an objective. This will also vary by leadership style and by the level of confidence they have in the employee(s) to be followed up with.

POINTS TO PONDER — SOMETHING TO THINK ABOUT

1. In the past, how have you developed your objectives? Were they clearly defined and obtainable?
2. What standards did you employ to create definable and obtainable objectives? Explain.

TRAINING ACTIVITY — APPLICATION & ACTION PLAN

1. Develop a planning mechanism to create definable and attainable objectives for each goal you must accomplish.
2. Involve employees in the following steps:
    - List
    - Prioritize
    - Assign responsibility
    - Assign resources and budget
    - Create a timeline and milestones
    - Develop performance standards
    - Develop reporting and follow up procedures

5

Establishing Performance Standards

Performance plans are action plans, not static documents. Effective performance plans must detail the specific actions leaders and employees must follow to accomplish the goals and objectives set within it. Leaders understand that without meaningful performance standards, measuring and evaluating individual performance becomes difficult if not impossible. Once the plan is implemented, meaningful performance standards allow leaders to modify and adapt their plans to actual conditions.

Leaders must use solid standards to monitor and evaluate all aspects of performance. Any measurement used should determine and create an action both on the part of the employee being evaluated and on the part of the leader performing the evaluation.

IMPLICATIONS — WHAT THIS MEANS TO YOU

There is a natural tendency for a leader to focus his or her activities on more prominent areas that will be highlighted and spotlighted, yet every element of the performance plan must be fully addressed.

It should be noted that any standard a leader creates will direct, limit and change the behavior and performance of their employees. This is important for leaders to understand because what and how they choose to evaluate can have either a positive or negative effect on the performance of their organizational unit.

A common pitfall in establishing performance standards is overdoing them. It burdens all involved with excessive factors and controls. Leaders know that to be effective, they need to set performance standards that are relevant and meaningful. It is far better to have fewer meaningful standards than to establish many useless ones. When applied, these standards will present a true picture of the performance of their organizational unit at any given point in time. Four areas to focus on in creating meaningful performance standards are:

What to Measure

The specific elements that need to be measured will vary by organizational unit. Typically, performance standards are set around productivity and profitability. Most leaders establish performance standards by setting specific performance expectations. Examples include:

- Progress is evaluated by the reaching of specific milestones linked to individual goals and objectives.
- Profitability is evaluated against the budgets established for each activity.
- Efficiency is evaluated by the resource utilization within the organizational unit.

Each organizational unit has key factors that determine their success. Leaders identify these factors as indicators of performance and look for trigger points that are early indicators of the success or failure of these factors. For instance, if a leader is managing a manufacturing unit, he or she may focus on projected orders as a key indicator of their unit's future activities. While a production supervisor may not be interested in these future indicators, a leader looks beyond the immediate horizon to maximize the efficiency of their unit.

How to Benchmark

Once leaders know what they want to evaluate, they need to benchmark each critical measurement. This establishes degrees of confidence and reliability in their numbers. They review these statistics over a meaningful period of time to establish a benchmark of past performance in each area. The longer a leader reviews the past performance of a specific area, the higher the degree of confidence and reliability he or she establishes.

Once key performance standards are benchmarked, leaders establish "triggering events" that result in taking immediate action. Since the benchmarked statistic is the standard, a triggering event can be predetermined. This event or "flag" occurs when performance rises above or falls below a specific percentage of the benchmarked standard. This provides leaders an early warning system to proactively deal with performance problems before they get out of hand.

How Frequently to Measure

Leaders are careful not to overburden themselves with needless information. They use performance standards as a means to keep their finger on the pulse of their unit's performance. They can easily determine the frequency for receiving reports of their unit's performance. Some statistics are meaningful on a daily basis, some hourly, and still others only when reported over prolonged periods of time.

What Measurements Indicate

Key performance standards need to inform leaders of the overall performance of their organizational unit. Specific measurements can trigger corrective actions, while others indicate the progress of the unit against performance plan goals and objectives. Effectively utilized, solid performance standards lead and direct the leader's actions to fine-tune his or her unit's performance. The right balance of key standards points the way to improved overall performance and productivity.

POINTS TO PONDER — SOMETHING TO THINK ABOUT

1. How have you used performance standards to assist in effectively leading your organizational unit?
2. Have you been static or proactive in the use of performance standards?

TRAINING ACTIVITY — APPLICATION & ACTION PLAN

1. Since the needs and specifications of each organizational unit vary, identify the key factors defining your unit's success.
2. Determine how to measure and quantify its key factors.
3. Identify how to benchmark these numbers by using past performance statistics.
4. Identify specific triggering events that warn of potential performance problems.
5. Determine what information needs to be reported and how frequently.
6. Identify what your measurements indicate and what actions or activities each one will trigger.

6

Monitoring Performance Against Actual Results

When a leader develops and refines their performance plan, it becomes their active leadership tool to guide and direct their activities throughout the year. As specific events and circumstances change, leaders know they must adapt in order to maintain their effectiveness and productivity.

While many mangers react to circumstances and events that impact their areas of responsibility, leaders anticipate and act proactively. Acting proactively minimizes any negative impact on their organizational unit. It allows them to maintain their projected levels of profitability and productivity. Effective leaders keep their finger on the pulse of their unit's activities. They understand the need to direct and motivate, and resist the urge to actively interfere in the activities of their employees.

IMPLICATIONS – WHAT THIS MEANS TO YOU

Leaders need to remain objective in order to be effective. While involvement with employees is desirable to encourage, direct and correct their activities, leaders must be able to maintain a degree of distance that gives them a vantage point from which to oversee the total performance of their organizational unit.

STRATEGIES, TIPS & TECHNIQUES TO APPLY

Leaders understand there is a logical progression of activities that flows from their performance plans. At the highest levels, performance plans determine the overall goals and objectives for the year. From this flows the roles, tasks and assignments that insure the goals and objectives are met for the year. These are scheduled throughout the year. Performance standards and specific triggering events are then linked to each task, assignment and responsibility. Every activity is linked to the successful completion of the other.

The role of the leader, once the plans are developed and implemented, is to motivate, monitor, direct and correct all employees' activities. This ensures the successful completion of the performance plan. This includes adjusting and adapting plans to actual conditions, circumstances and events that impact the performance of the plan.

The most effective techniques to maintain control over the organizational unit's activities include:

Development of Management Metrics

Effective leaders continually make use of metrics to gauge the ongoing performance of their unit's activities. Corporations have the ability to generate a great deal of data and information for their managers. Rather than being overburdened by needless data, leaders are able to distill the information provided to them. They convert this information into a series of meaningful statistics or metrics that help them stay on top of their unit's performance.

While each organizational unit's key numbers will vary, some of the common metrics used include sales, accounts receivable, units produced, inventory, payables and production hours. Astute leaders generate a single page report once or twice daily providing them with the key metrics for their organizational unit. These generally summarize key performance activities. A secondary report is made available if the leader wishes to examine any details of a specific problem or when a triggering event occurs. In this fashion, leaders stay on top of their units.

The metrics report may vary as additional measurements are reported on a weekly or monthly basis. Most managers can have IT generate specific and meaningful metrics reports.

Ability to Adapt to Change

The use of effective metrics is only a compass guiding the direction of the organizational unit. Leaders use them to make directional changes and modifications, to keep the unit focused and on course. Metrics may also indicate the need to work with and/or coach specific employees to eliminate negative behaviors or barriers to performance.

The role of a leader is to maintain control and to focus on fine-tuning his or her organization to sustain and achieve the desired level of performance and productivity.

Responding to Triggering Events

As discussed earlier, leaders establish trigger points that predict potential problems and issues before they fully impact the organizational unit. Effective leaders also establish contingency plans for each of their triggering events. These outline exactly what to do when such an event occurs.

The initial step is to define the triggering event and understand what it means when it occurs. As it is an immediate call for action, leaders must determine the specific strategies and actions that need to be taken when these events occur. They also delegate and train selected employees to handle these situations if they cannot be present or available to take charge over them.

Leaders understand problems will occur, and thus prepare for them. The second aspect of the contingency plan is to determine the resources needed to handle an occurring problem. This includes developing a trained response team equipped with the necessary physical resources to deal directly with the problem.

POINTS TO PONDER — SOMETHING TO THINK ABOUT

1. How do you monitor the performance of your organizational unit?
2. Do you continually take the pulse of the key activities in all your various areas of responsibility?

TRAINING ACTIVITY — APPLICATION & ACTION PLAN

1. Determine the key metrics or statistics you need to have in order to maintain active control and leadership over your organizational unit.
2. Identify what specific numbers should be reported to you and in what frequency.
3. Create contingency plans for each triggering event your metrics indicate.

7

Starved for Knowledge

Leaders are awash in data and information but starve for knowledge. Information is useless unless it readily provides the leader with key insights that allow him or her to apply their expertise to solve a problem, resolve an issue or improve performance. Additionally, too much information can hinder a leader's ability to effectively lead their organization.

IMPLICATIONS – WHAT THIS MEANS TO YOU

As corporations grow, they tend to become bureaucratic. Individuals generate reams of reports and forms to justify their position and importance. Some managers hide their inefficiency behind mountains of reports and data. Effective leaders are able to rise above this sea of information and distill it into a series of key metrics and reports. This effort provides them with the knowledge needed to manage their areas of responsibility.

This is important for leaders to understand because it is too easy to get bogged down in meetings and reports that don't contribute to their productivity and profitability. Leaders use information to their advantage but cast off the burdens of needless information that hinder their ability to lead.

STRATEGIES, TIPS & TECHNIQUES TO APPLY

Leaders are able to filter through the bureaucratic sea of information to obtain the specific data and reports they need to effectively manage their activities and organizational unit. They are able to do this by using the following techniques:

Knowing What Is Being Reported and Available

Leaders know what is being reported throughout the corporation and what is available to them. They are able to filter out the reports and information they need to receive. They cancel or delegate other reports to subordinates to analyze for them.

Knowing What Information Is Needed

Leaders know what critical sections or numbers in a report they need to access. Where possible, they use subordinates to generate a simple one-page summary of the information they need to effectively lead and manage their organization. If necessary, they refer to the full reports for additional detail. They understand that delegation frees up their time and ability to effectively lead. This action also allows subordinates to professionally develop critical skills.

Knowing What the Information Reports

Effective leaders ensure they are provided with precise information and data they require to efficiently lead and manage their organization. They also know what every metric means to them at a single glance, gauging whether performance is increasing or lagging. When necessary, they know where to go to obtain the supporting data and analysis required, to assist them to pinpoint problematic areas of performance.

Knowing How Often Information Should Be Received

Effective leaders know the frequency when specific information needs to be reported to them. They know what information they need to have at their fingertips and what can be periodically reported to them. They understand that timeliness of specific information is essential to their success. They also know that information reported too frequently is as hindering as having too much information.

Knowing What to Do with the Information

Effective leaders know what to do with the information they receive and what events and activities each piece of information and data triggers within their organization. They clearly understand what the information means to them and how they need to apply it.

Knowing What Will Happen if Information Is Not Received

Leaders understand that there is certain information that is essential to effectively direct and lead their organizations. They also wisely know that a great deal of information will never be missed if they never receive it. Unessential information is delegated to subordinates or eliminated all together.

Knowing How to Maximize Time by Minimizing Information

Information can take many forms besides reports. Many leaders are needlessly copied letters, faxes and emails by subordinates. More are included in countless meetings. Effective leaders learn how to delegate and eliminate many sources of unnecessary information. They understand this works to hamper their ability to effectively lead and manage their organizations. If their presence is requested at a meeting, they assign a subordinate to represent them or turn down the request if their presence is not totally necessary.

Effective leaders understand that a specific amount of information is required to manage the organization. Anything above that level is a needless burden. If they allow it, an oversaturation of information decreases their effectiveness and productivity. They use their expertise, wisdom and experience to distinguish between the information they need to know and the information that carries little or no value to their efforts.

POINTS TO PONDER – SOMETHING TO THINK ABOUT

1. Do you personally feel overwhelmed by the amount of information and data you receive on a regular basis?
2. How do you currently handle all of the information you receive? Do you feel it hinders your performance and effectiveness?

TRAINING ACTIVITY – APPLICATION & ACTION PLAN

1. Examine the reports, data and information you receive on a regular basis from associates and subordinates.
2. Determine the information you actually require to effective lead your organizational unit.
3. Where possible, delegate or eliminate the information that does not directly contribute to your effectiveness as a leader.
4. Meet with your subordinates to determine ways they can assist you to filter through and provide a meaningful summary of the information you need on a regular basis.
5. Eliminate any information, correspondence and meetings that do not directly contribute to your effectiveness in moving your organizational unit forward to the accomplishment of its goals and objectives.

8

Adapting Performance Plans to Change

Managers often fear change and its consequences. Leaders embrace change and seek ways to maximize its opportunities. Effective leaders keep their eyes on the horizon and scan for trends and events potentially impacting their areas of responsibility. Scanning for trends allows leaders to minimize the disruption change can cause in their organization.

Technological advances over the years have fueled wave after wave of change repeatedly impacting corporations. This has proven the inevitability of change and allowed leaders to approach it with the flexibility needed to adapt and survive. When a company is resistant to change, the organization is often placed at risk and the bottom line negatively impacted.

IMPLICATIONS — WHAT THIS MEANS TO YOU

Managers as leaders must recognize how and why specific changes can damage their organization if not dealt with properly. A leader anticipates impending change, and plans accordingly to minimize its effect. Proper planning allows companies to adapt by shedding unproductive elements while adding others to capitalize on market shifts. Leaders maintain an open mind to adapt their performance plans to inevitable changes.

When developing and finalizing annual performance plans, leaders take the necessary steps to plan for any and all anticipated changes. They also make contingency plans for unanticipated or undisclosed events. These are occurrences that might impact the plan's success as well as the overall performance of the organization.

Recent events have demonstrated how quickly circumstances can change. Since leaders are proactive rather than reactive, they are always thinking ahead and anticipating how they can improve their organization's performance. They do this in four ways:

Welcoming Change

Leaders welcome the opportunities change brings. They are optimistic about how change opens previously closed or unexplored avenues, and the results they can achieve through these new routes. This is in direct contrast to managers who shrink from change, who are inflexible and comfortable in their positions. They perceive change as a threat, and myopically overlook the opportunities it presents.

Anticipating Change

Leaders know change is inevitable. They are always aware of their circumstances and how things may be transforming and evolving around them. Once they identify an emerging trend or change, they take immediate action to ensure their organization quickly adapts to it. This often minimizes the impact and disruptions that change can bring to their organizational unit.

Using Performance Standards and Measurements

Performance standards and measurements are management tools that guide and direct leaders throughout the year. They know these metrics are merely indicators of actions and activities that need to be pursued. Leaders have preplanned contingencies for most events detailing specific actions and strategies. They are aware of the strengths and weaknesses of their subordinates and organizational unit. Because of this, they are prepared to make modifications and corrections to balance the performance of the entire unit. Shifting personnel and resources to counter changes and resolve problems becomes a top priority. This helps a leader to maintain a flexible posture that allows him or her to move quickly if required.

Anticipating Uncontrollable Events and Trends

Every organization and corporation is subject to outside influences and events. These include the effects of economy, weather and industry trends and changes. Some of these cannot be predicted, but many can be anticipated.

In formulating performance plans, effective leaders go through a series of "what if" scenarios. These identify a number of uncontrollable events. They examine economic, industrial and, if applicable, weather trends to determine whether anything on the horizon might affect their organizational unit's performance. While this planning is not done with any level of certainty, leaders act as sentries, constantly keeping an eye to future events in anticipation of potential problems/opportunities. This allows them to put initial contingency plans into place, then take them full-scale once the probability of these events occurring increases.

POINTS TO PONDER – SOMETHING TO THINK ABOUT

1. What is your personal attitude toward change? Do you embrace it or are you fearful of its consequences?
2. Do you anticipate and plan for change or do you negatively react to it when it occurs?

TRAINING ACTIVITY – APPLICATION & ACTION PLAN

1. Identify any anticipated or unanticipated changes, uncontrollable events or trends that could directly impact your areas of responsibilities.
2. Determine what your response to each change will be.
3. Identify the trigger points when you should take action.
4. Develop contingency plans for each major event.
    - What will you do?
    - What changes or modifications will you need to make?
    - Who will be involved?
    - What resources will you need?
    - How long will it take?

About the Author

Timothy F. Bednarz, Ph.D. is CEO of the American Management Development Group, Inc. For over 20 years he has researched, designed and authored hundreds of learning and development programs used by Fortune 1000 companies.

He is also the author of *Great! What Makes Leaders Great. What They Did, How They Did It and What You Can Learn from It* (2011).

Speaking Availability

Timothy F. Bednarz, Ph.D. is available for speaking engagements for your next meeting or association event. He can be contacted at 800-654-4935 or by e-mail at timothy.bednarz@majorium.com.

Bulk Sales

Bulk sales of this book or any other titles available from Majorium Business Press. Inquiries can be directed to sales@majorium.com, or by phone at 800-6654-4935.

Quick Order Form

Fax orders: 715-342-1118. Send this form.

Telephone orders: Call 800-654-4935 toll-free. Have your credit card ready.

Email orders: sales@majorium.com

Postal orders: Majorium Business Press, 2025 Main Street, Stevens Point, WI 54481, USA.

Please send the following books:

____

____

____

____

Please send more FREE information on:

❑Catalog ❑Speaking/Seminars ❑Mailing Lists ❑Consulting

Name: ____________________________________

Address: __________________________________

City: ____________________ State: _____ Zip: __________

Telephone: ________________________________

Email address: ______________________________

Sales tax: Please add 5.5% for products shipped to Wisconsin addresses.

Shipping by air:

United States: $4.00 for first book and $2.00 for each additional product.

International: $9.00 for first book; $5.00 for each additional product (estimate).

Made in United States
Cleveland, OH
05 November 2026

47675527R00030